Shadows Beneath the Moon

Ivan Collado

BookLeaf Publishing

India | USA | UK

Presentation by *BookLeaf Publishing*

Web: www.bookleafpub.com

E-mail: info@bookleafpub.com

ISBN: 9789363301528

First edition 2024

ACKNOWLEDGEMENT

Sincere gratitude towards the band HEKCETERA for their inspirational content and viewpoints that assisted in the creation of this book. Absolutely love all of them! Check them out on Spotify!

PREFACE

Shadows Beneath the Moon is a poetry book detailing the transition of human-to-vampire in a vivid and mesmerizing way. It is a poetic story inspired by a love for fantasy, romance, and of course, vampires.

Enjoy a new way of embracing the vampire-genre through way of story telling that'll take your breath away.

Ordinary, Act I

The morning peered,
Through jade curtains,
As exhaustion held firmly my body,

Alarm blaring,
The snooze too far from my fingertips,
And oddly enough,
My dry lips were aching for a drink.

Another ten minutes passed,
Because I blinked once for too long,
And woke up a little later,

The world was normal,
Judging by the tweeting and rustling sounds of
nature
Thus I would be late for school.

Ordinary, Act II

Elizabeth was a common name to common
people,
Engraved into royal families,
Creating royal sequels and for me,
It was more unique than an alignment of
snowflakes on a winter's day,
Analyzing patterns at night to stay awake,

She captivated me.

I woke strictly for her,
There was something about her,
Something in her voice,
That was all too alluring,
She conjured tranquil notes with embedded
hope,
That left my fragile heart churning,

Love or lust, to tell I could not,
Every part of me wants to dive deep into the
warmth of every crevice,
To hold you close and kiss you hard,
While lifting your leg and,
Simultaneously hearing about your day.

Ordinary, Act III

The bellowing of drums
Musical tempest of wind instruments
Layered with,
All-consuming passion in action,
Perspiring from having their emotions happen,
In the form of beautiful notes.
The volume and depth of the universe,
Expands with hues,
Reminding me of,
The happiness of my youth.
Fulfilled, everlasting
Brimming with an eternity of love
For everything around me.
Like the flowers beneath the kiss of summer.

Love Letter

My desk had been filled with pens and pencils,
Erasers and sharpeners,
Notes and folders,
Not intending to hold her
Emotions underneath the disaster of my careless
collections
Upon inspection,
There had been laughter aimed this way from
countless directions
Perhaps, I sat in someone else's fecal weapon
I should mention it isn't the first time I was
made to sit in shit that someone else had
discarded with
But this time it was different.
I just went with it
And I followed this
Odd idea that there was more to my desk that
met the eye
Swimming through the clutter and having caught
my eye
A letter to me, I was surprised
That it was stickered by…
You.
Elizabeth. Had this been a prank of our
classroom?

Were you in on it too?
To meet after school had awaited the tail-end of
a school year joke
Yet, I couldn't help but take the chance
For my battered heart is no more than a
candlewick lit with hope.

Under the Moon

The contents of the letter
Took common sense left severed
From my brainstem despite the weather
Of the tornado ravaging the strings of my heart
Anxiety had become my circuitry and wires
My mask depicted I was not even a shred tired
If anything, it said I was happy
And I was, but wasn't
School ending bells hadn't sounded so rich
And also redundant
I waited for you.
Elizabeth, after school like you had mentioned
There you were
Beside a tree towering in height
Beneath the splitting lines of daytime light
Shimmering in the summer glow
Alone.
Awkward at first,
Your initiative occurred, with you pulling my
hand to yours
We've known each other for how long,
Too long, yet you knew all along
How funny I was?
How kind I was?
How smart I was?

You didn't hesitate to freely speak of my
character
That when you stood quiet and it had then
become my turn
I couldn't utter a single word.
You caught on and your face flushed red
So instead, you said there was a party tonight
and you'd like if I came too
For there'd be a moment you'd like to share with
me
Us two,
Under the moon.

Transition, Act I

Eyes open,
Like any normal day void of shadow
Yet waking in the pits of hell to church bells,
Head Ringing, lost as to where I've traveled
Bourbon drinks hadn't cut the link,
To my mind, as swiftly as the night prior
Stumbled to my feet, crunching rocks
No soul in sight nor billboard clocks
Blood stained upon my attire

Heart-thumping, mind stumping,
Nauseating clumps of anxiety dumping
Onto my shoulders and I,
Fall back to the bark of Mother Nature
Restless in my forgetfulness
And wondering what happened.

Transition, Act II

Trembling,
Madness had corrupted the crown,
Now I wear it.

The red cracks barreled through the whites of
my eye,
Now I hear it,

Pulsating,
Like a soft, reverberating knock on wood doors,
Increasingly louder, and louder,
To rough pounds across the marble floors,
My fingernails scraping at bare skin
Encasing anxiety in fractured brain stems and,
I screamed.

Their hearts pumped,
With a sound that held me by the throat
I loathed,
Being choked by nothing physically tangible,
but mentally repressing

Yet, there I was,
Undressing folks with my eyes,
Not just their clothes,

But their skin,
Not just their bones,
All down to the red nectar, and I hope,
There was a logical answer to the question,
Why did I want to kill?

Transition, Act III

 I wonder for what reason do I stare at you,
Frozen in a still frame of eternal pain,
Knowing that you aren't mine.
Yet, you could be.

It was in my absent-mind that I longed to find
you,
At my doorstep,
And for some reason, you were there.
Elizabeth,
Why
Are
You
 Here?

The rain pounded into my feeble windows,
Your shadow stretched over the floorboards,
Worried, now worried no more,
As you tore from the door and forward to me
It was perfect.
Despite the circumstances having yearned for
this,
Endless, or so I prayed to never end this.
Your kind heart protected everyone
But your words, they fell on deaf ears,

Drowned by the succulent sound of your blood,
Pumping, escalating the fear
My hands shook,
Mouth parched,
Breath ragged,
You were warm with smooth skin,
A fragrance too, a new perfume,
A top that hung a little too loose,
And a body, voluptuous
I wanted nothing more than to,
With all respect,
Push you away and scream danger.
In my arms, you were no longer safer,
Than you would be at home,
The demons have built this space,
Leaving no longer a trace,
Of the man you knew,
Elizabeth, you must run.
But I blinked and,
You became the sweetest treat my lips have
pressed upon.
And everything went black.

Love Bite

Ecstasy,
Your velvet skin was delicate,
Every inch was bathed within,
The cherry blossoms,
A fragrance that left each of my hairs standing,
Every doubt left abandoned
A sweet nectar that escaped punctured holes
Hands caressing your supple body
Till heart holes turnt to heart whole
Your love was a binding spell,
Trickling past my lips to distant dreams of
wedding bells
Life has never had more meaning,
For if this were the encapsulating bliss
Of a thousand twists,
On our journey to overcome all overarching
risks
Destined shackles never felt more freeing
In my gentle hands,
You moan and you whimper,
You squeeze and you quiver,
Without the need,
To unbuckle or unzipper
Red had been your color,
In your beautiful yet fading eyes,
Going under.

The Way Your Body Fell

Your eyes shut their final chapter,
As the pleasure died thereafter,
Your smile faded as your whole life shattered,
As did mine,
Falling hold to demonic captors,
Your neck slung to the side,
Your fingers lost their strength,
Once gripping my blood-stained shirt,
Fading fast upon your final breath
My fangs rested centimeters above your ravaged
neck
As my breath left shaken,
My heart now devil-sent,
Elizabeth, talk to me.
Your legs buckled,
My body lunged forward,
Squeezing you close to my chest,
Cupping your soft cheek in my hand
My blurred eyes searing from the volcanic flow
of water streaming down my face and like you, I
couldn't stand
Together, we fell.
One breathing, the other not.
Sickening,
I screamed out to the world,

I didn't mean it.
Elizabeth, you see that? Right?
Your soul tied to the light,
As the heavens reeled you in,
And I cried,
Weeping,
Beneath the lights of a home,
Seeping,
Between the crevices of my livelihood
Fading in color down to your favorite shade of
gray
Dreaming
That I could turn back time to before we met
Maybe then, this monster you see
Wouldn't have been the monster you get

Forsaken in the Heat, Act I

Purposeful isolation,
Hours out of seconds
Confessions, suppression
Resurrections, this perception
Of life, bringing souls back from heaven
In my aggression, broken walls
Had been lessons, an obsession
Inflicting self-harm for redemption
Crayon-marks across the halls
Were an extension of my mental health
Desiring therapeutic sessions
To stabilize myself
Turning deeper to hell
As the sun peered through my window
Over Elizabeth,
Burning my hand,
Me pulling away
Leaving a blistering red mark that healed
As quickly as it scorched.

Forsaken in the Heat, Act II

You were the sun in my life,
Just as I had forsaken you,
The sun had forsaken me,
It beamed, stronger than ever
It burned, just by the touch
It disfigured, my skin so I'd remember
The slaughter of eternal love
What was happening to me?
And if my body could not bear the light no more
Let night be my fortress
And with you, well…
What should I do with you, Elizabeth?

Forsaken in the Heat, Act III

Your body still laid on the middle of my
floorboards,
Your spine-curdling stench like a raging banshee
that sought not my nose, but my eyes
My veiny pupils distraught and turned
Toward the corner of walls where darkness lied
Come night, Elizabeth, you shall leave.
The moon, eventually, slithered above the
horizon
And I slithered, too, as your body I had to hide it
Wrapped in fine leather, with one finger
protruding out
Thrown into the back of the trunk and in silence
I'd shout
I'd sit as the driver, throw my fist to the wheel,
I'd kick into the plastic, how could anyone know
how it feels
To mourn love and to be entirely rejuvenated by
their death.
Regretfully, replenished.
Her body crashed into the clear waters far in the
distance
Raising waves, and there I stayed, watching her
sink as the only eye witness
Knowing,
I'd have to live with this.

One Bullet Less

The single round went into my temple,
Out the other end,
All I saw was dark.
A gap in time, the world clicked rewind
I woke up with a beating heart.
No matter how many times this trigger is pulled,
Or other ways I'd try to end,
It didn't matter what I'd do,
For I always wake up hours later,
With just one bullet less.

What Happened Beneath the Moon?

Face stubble,
Stink, like sweat and mop water
These dark bags, sinister black moons beneath
pupils
Repugnant tongue with white cheese smeared
teeth
Corner room, bleached floors, I just couldn't
believe—
My wrist glimmered for just a second,
As if it were a gentle tweet from heaven,
But it was no more than a bracelet of vague
memories.
Plastic string tied rubies
With no receipt
Nor recollection on when this gift had been
received
It faded and blinked in, snippets of television
static and human skins, cheap liquor and mild
panic, grassy meadows and drugged out addicts,
over the hill and through white roses, never an
end or at least an end seemed hopeless
Then it stopped.
Every vision in my head, see it had been a lot
Of things, I vaguely remembered.

Pieces of a night that part of me didn't want to
lose
Without the only person able to tell me
Elizabeth, why didn't you tell me
What exactly happened beneath the moon?

Time to Myself

A friend dialed,
Asking if I'd been okay
He hadn't heard in weeks and when he asked,
No one could say,
Exactly where I'd been.
I ignored his message.
He showed up the next day.
His fists were worried hammers trying to break
down the door
I stood with my back to it.
The shaking wood jolsting the bones in my
body.
My heart—
I could feel it.
A heavy beat.
Heavy emotions.
I couldn't grasp whether or not I had been scared
of the sun
Or scared of what I'd say should the door open.
Or what I'd do.
David's veins had been a goldmine.
My fangs were the tool.
I am already a murderer, David.
Don't take away my ability to choose.
Stay away.

The Text

My fingers treaded where my brain was too
afraid to travel
Cellular devices renowned for their use during a
crisis,
Having a way with words and submerging many
to five second death grips
Meanwhile I was afraid to come to terms with
No longer seeing your name, hearts and all,
inside a bubble pop up on the front screen, I had
seen the way our emojis exchanged,
Like a bouquet of flowers with more than one
face
And sunset photography to encapsulate the
beautiful day.
I knew what I really wanted.
Not just you, but answers.
Who I was
What I became
What happened that night
Where everything changed
The one piece to a puzzle that long disturbed my
slumber
Had began with the text, an address
345 Hunter.

Danger to All

Hunter.
Synonymous with killer,
Gunshots and open wounds,
Home had been a safe space
But not for whom
The Hunter hunted.
My strength was tenfold.
My speed would match.
An uncontrollable hunger
No one safe from its path
Hence why when I arrived under
The oak trees of 345 Hunter
I was left breathless.
Two kids and a mother.
Playing outside at night during summer
To what had I been walking into, Elizabeth?
Discovery of my new nature,
Rested behind the walls of domestic labor
Was there a savior hiding behind the blinds?
Or had I just been blind to the irony of this street
name
A universal sign that my new nature would
never change
But I had to find out.
If not for me, then for you

Because at this point, what did I have to lose?
One foot forward,
Three heads turned.

Innocent Lives

Their fear hadn't been much,
Just a trickle of sweat down their cheeks.
Their confusion had been a lot
With wide eyes that spoke to me
A mother bear, steadfast and fierce
Her instincts were as sharp as mine
For two entirely different reasons.
She asked who I was,
A question I danced around
I asked about a party that she must've known
about
For it took place here.
Within the amber walls of her home
The lady asked me to leave.
I told her I won't.
She said she'd call the cops.
For their sake, please don't.
Fear had held her by the collar, enticing her to
remain still
My breath, as foul as it had been, left her nose
with such a chill
I could hear the blood rush beneath her skin.
The party, I asked again.
She told her two youngest to step inside,
And I followed all three of them in.

A Name We All Remembered

You knew Elizabeth,
She once dated your eldest son.
The man invited her over
To a party he begun
Absence with a lapse in judgment
You've been a mother to two,
Forgetful to the first child you had
The distance between you two grew
You weren't home at the time,
Your trust in him had been that of shield to soldier
That he would age like fine wine, better when older
I knew not of your son, but I knew of circumstance
The gravity of isolation
The desecration towards the mind of man
Yet, the answer to my question had remained elusive
The truth is,
I am what no human wants to be.
And I think your son knows what happened to me.

Floating Under the Moon

Your hands held the throat of a gun as if it had
been my own,
Your mouth spat slurs historically hurt as if
you'd been in the room alone,
Your children hid behind you as if that divide
would further raise the hope
That these fangs of mine would then turn shy
and conceal the danger that I posed
Edward had been a good child,
The name of your eldest I presumed,
One night he came home different,
No one knew what to do.
No one else would be hurt,
No other lives the world would lose
You'd keep him contained
But that was the light that lit the fuse
It was too late.
My nails scraped into my palm
A natural growl escaped my lips
One bullet, two, then three
Because Mother Bear must protect her kids
My body slumped like a sandbag to the floor,
Blackness all consuming
Waking to the television sounds in an empty
house,

My trembling body followed the sound
The news had been on,
Volume maxed out,
Floating under the moon,
A body had been found.